YOU CAN MAKE

DeafWelcome

Learn American Sign Language

VONNY SHOTZ
Photography

Picture Credits
Cover, Vonny Shotz Photography
Signing Model, Theressa DuBois
Maymont Park, Richmond, VA

Copyright © 2015 Deaf Welcome Foundation
All rights reserved. No part of this book may be used or reproduced or transmitted in any form or by any means, electronic or mechanical, including photocopying, or by any information storage and retrieval system, without written permission of the publisher.

For information regarding permission to make copies of any part of this book, write to Deaf Welcome Foundation, 501(c)(3) National Charity for Sign Language TV, Media & Film, P.O. Box 3431, Richmond, VA 23235.

Printed in the United States of America

ISBN-13: 978-1514236901
ISBN-10: 1514236907

American Sign Language (ASL) is not universal.
ASL is the third largest language used in the United States.
There are *many* signed languages around the world.
So, let's get you started with some basic signs.
You can begin making Deaf welcome
in your community, today.

DEDICATED TO THE

Gonzalez Family

Ms. Bailey, Ms. Burch, Ms. Charity,

and *X*

with love

YOU CAN MAKE *DeafWelcome*
Learn American Sign Language

Name
Nombre

√	Look for opportunities to sign with the Deaf and Hard-of-hearing. Check when done.	Busque oportunidades firmar con los sordos. Comprobar cuando termine.
☐	Deaf School	Escuela del Sordos
☐	Deaf Church	Iglesia del Sordos
☐	My school	Mi escuela
☐	My job	Mi trabajo
☐	My church	Mi iglesia
☐	Meeting	Reunión
☐	Party	Fiesta
☐	Special Event	Especial
☐	Emergency	Emergencia
☐	My Event	De mí

YOU CAN MAKE *Deaf Welcome*

Learn American Sign Language

Dad • Padre

YOU CAN MAKE *DeafWelcome*

How did you use this sign with the Deaf?
¿Cómo se utiliza esta señal con los sordos?

Explain • Explica

_____

_____

_____

_____

_____

_____

(√) Check when done
Terminado

YOU CAN MAKE *DeafWelcome*

Learn American Sign Language

Mom • Madre

YOU CAN MAKE *DeafWelcome*

How did you use this sign with the Deaf?
¿Cómo se utiliza esta señal con los sordos?

Explain • Explica

_____

_____

_____

_____

_____

_____

(√) Check when done
Terminado

YOU CAN MAKE *Deaf Welcome*

Learn American Sign Language

yes • sí

YOU CAN MAKE *DeafWelcome*

How did you use this sign with the Deaf?
¿Cómo se utiliza esta señal con los sordos?

Explain • Explica

_____

_____

_____

_____

_____

_____

☐ (√) Check when done
Terminado

YOU CAN MAKE *Deaf Welcome*

Learn American Sign Language

no

YOU CAN MAKE *DeafWelcome*

How did you use this sign with the Deaf?
¿Cómo se utiliza esta señal con los sordos?

Explain • Explica

_____

_____

_____

_____

_____

_____

_____

(√) Check when done
Terminado

YOU CAN MAKE *Deaf Welcome*

Learn American Sign Language

please • por favor

YOU CAN MAKE *DeafWelcome*

How did you use this sign with the Deaf?
¿Cómo se utiliza esta señal con los sordos?

Explain • Explica

_____

_____

_____

_____

_____

_____

☐ (√) Check when done
   Terminado

YOU CAN MAKE *Deaf Welcome*

Learn American Sign Language

thank you • gracías

YOU CAN MAKE *DeafWelcome*

How did you use this sign with the Deaf?
¿Cómo se utiliza esta señal con los sordos?

Explain • Explica

(√) Check when done
Terminado

YOU CAN MAKE *Deaf Welcome*

Learn American Sign Language

sorry • lo siento

YOU CAN MAKE *DeafWelcome*

How did you use this sign with the Deaf?
¿Cómo se utiliza esta señal con los sordos?

Explain • Explica

_____

_____

_____

_____

_____

_____

☐ (√) Check when done
Terminado

YOU CAN MAKE *Deaf Welcome*

Learn American Sign Language

bathroom • baño

YOU CAN MAKE *DeafWelcome*

How did you use this sign with the Deaf?
¿Cómo se utiliza esta señal con los sordos?

Explain • Explica

(√) Check when done
Terminado

YOU CAN MAKE *Deaf Welcome*

Learn American Sign Language

understand • comprender

YOU CAN MAKE *DeafWelcome*

How did you use this sign with the Deaf?
¿Cómo se utiliza esta señal con los sordos?

Explain • Explica

(√) Check when done
Terminado

YOU CAN MAKE *Deaf Welcome*

Learn American Sign Language

help • ayudar

YOU CAN MAKE *DeafWelcome*

How did you use this sign with the Deaf?
¿Cómo se utiliza esta señal con los sordos?

Explain • Explica

(√) Check when done
Terminado

YOU CAN MAKE *Deaf Welcome*

Learn American Sign Language

true • verdad

YOU CAN MAKE *DeafWelcome*

How did you use this sign with the Deaf?
¿Cómo se utiliza esta señal con los sordos?

Explain • Explica

(√) Check when done
Terminado

YOU CAN MAKE *Deaf Welcome*

Learn American Sign Language

false • falso(a)

YOU CAN MAKE *DeafWelcome*

How did you use this sign with the Deaf?
¿Cómo se utiliza esta señal con los sordos?

Explain • Explica

_____

_____

_____

_____

_____

_____

☐ (√) Check when done
    Terminado

YOU CAN MAKE *Deaf Welcome*

Learn American Sign Language

lie • mentira

YOU CAN MAKE *DeafWelcome*

How did you use this sign with the Deaf?
¿Cómo se utiliza esta señal con los sordos?

Explain • Explica

_____

_____

_____

_____

_____

_____

(√) Check when done
Terminado

YOU CAN MAKE *Deaf Welcome*

Learn American Sign Language

need • necesitar

YOU CAN MAKE *DeafWelcome*

How did you use this sign with the Deaf?
¿Cómo se utiliza esta señal con los sordos?

Explain • Explica

_____

_____

_____

_____

_____

_____

(√) Check when done
Terminado

YOU CAN MAKE *Deaf Welcome*

Learn American Sign Language

want • querer

YOU CAN MAKE *DeafWelcome*

How did you use this sign with the Deaf?
¿Cómo se utiliza esta señal con los sordos?

Explain • Explica

_____

_____

_____

_____

_____

_____

(√) Check when done
Terminado

YOU CAN MAKE *Deaf Welcome*

Learn American Sign Language

happy • feliz

YOU CAN MAKE *DeafWelcome*

How did you use this sign with the Deaf?
¿Cómo se utiliza esta señal con los sordos?

Explain • Explica

(√) Check when done
Terminado

YOU CAN MAKE *Deaf* Welcome

Learn American Sign Language

sad • triste

YOU CAN MAKE *DeafWelcome*

How did you use this sign with the Deaf?
¿Cómo se utiliza esta señal con los sordos?

Explain • Explica

_____

_____

_____

_____

_____

_____

(√) Check when done
Terminado

YOU CAN MAKE *Deaf Welcome*

Learn American Sign Language

"ILY"

love • amor

YOU CAN MAKE *DeafWelcome*

How did you use this sign with the Deaf?
¿Cómo se utiliza esta señal con los sordos?

Explain • Explica

(√) Check when done
Terminado

YOU CAN MAKE *Deaf Welcome*

Learn American Sign Language

angry • enojado

YOU CAN MAKE *DeafWelcome*

How did you use this sign with the Deaf?
¿Cómo se utiliza esta señal con los sordos?

Explain • Explica

(√) Check when done
Terminado

YOU CAN MAKE *Deaf Welcome*

Learn American Sign Language

fun • divertido

YOU CAN MAKE *DeafWelcome*

How did you use this sign with the Deaf?
¿Cómo se utiliza esta señal con los sordos?

Explain • Explica

(√) Check when done
Terminado

YOU CAN MAKE *Deaf Welcome*

Learn American Sign Language

boring • aburrido(a)

YOU CAN MAKE *DeafWelcome*

How did you use this sign with the Deaf?
¿Cómo se utiliza esta señal con los sordos?

Explain • Explica

_____

_____

_____

_____

_____

_____

(√) Check when done
Terminado

YOU CAN MAKE *Deaf* Welcome

Learn American Sign Language

okay • bueno

YOU CAN MAKE *DeafWelcome*

How did you use this sign with the Deaf?
¿Cómo se utiliza esta señal con los sordos?

Explain • Explica

_____

_____

_____

_____

_____

_____

(√) Check when done
Terminado

YOU CAN MAKE *Deaf Welcome*

Learn American Sign Language

talk • hablar

YOU CAN MAKE *DeafWelcome*

How did you use this sign with the Deaf?
¿Cómo se utiliza esta señal con los sordos?

Explain • Explica

_____

_____

_____

_____

_____

_____

☐ (√) Check when done
Terminado

YOU CAN MAKE *Deaf Welcome*

Learn American Sign Language

stop • parar

YOU CAN MAKE *DeafWelcome*

How did you use this sign with the Deaf?
¿Cómo se utiliza esta señal con los sordos?

Explain • Explica

_____

_____

_____

_____

_____

_____

☐ (√) Check when done
Terminado

YOU CAN MAKE *Deaf Welcome*

Learn American Sign Language

go•ir

YOU CAN MAKE *DeafWelcome*

How did you use this sign with the Deaf?
¿Cómo se utiliza esta señal con los sordos?

Explain • Explica

_____

_____

_____

_____

_____

_____

(√) Check when done
Terminado

YOU CAN MAKE *Deaf Welcome*

Learn American Sign Language

good • bien

YOU CAN MAKE *DeafWelcome*

How did you use this sign with the Deaf?
¿Cómo se utiliza esta señal con los sordos?

Explain • Explica

_____

_____

_____

_____

_____

_____

☐　(√) Check when done
　　　　　　Terminado

YOU CAN MAKE *Deaf Welcome*

Learn American Sign Language

bad • mal

YOU CAN MAKE *DeafWelcome*

How did you use this sign with the Deaf?
¿Cómo se utiliza esta señal con los sordos?

Explain • Explica

(√) Check when done
Terminado

YOU CAN MAKE *Deaf Welcome*

Learn American Sign Language

left • izquierdo(a)

YOU CAN MAKE *DeafWelcome*

How did you use this sign with the Deaf?
¿Cómo se utiliza esta señal con los sordos?

Explain • Explica

___

___

___

___

___

___

(√) Check when done
Terminado

YOU CAN MAKE *Deaf Welcome*

Learn American Sign Language

right • derecho(a)

YOU CAN MAKE *DeafWelcome*

How did you use this sign with the Deaf?
¿Cómo se utiliza esta señal con los sordos?

Explain • Explica

(√) Check when done
Terminado

YOU CAN MAKE *Deaf Welcome*

Learn American Sign Language

right (correct) • correcto

YOU CAN MAKE *DeafWelcome*

How did you use this sign with the Deaf?
¿Cómo se utiliza esta señal con los sordos?

Explain • Explica

_____

_____

_____

_____

_____

_____

☐ (√) Check when done
Terminado

YOU CAN MAKE *Deaf Welcome*

Learn American Sign Language

wrong • incorrecto

YOU CAN MAKE *DeafWelcome*

How did you use this sign with the Deaf?
¿Cómo se utiliza esta señal con los sordos?

Explain • Explica

_____

_____

_____

_____

_____

_____

_____

☐   (√) Check when done
         Terminado

YOU CAN MAKE *Deaf Welcome*

Learn American Sign Language

schoolbus • autobús escolar

YOU CAN MAKE *DeafWelcome*

How did you use this sign with the Deaf?
¿Cómo se utiliza esta señal con los sordos?

Explain • Explica

_____

_____

_____

_____

_____

_____

☐ (√) Check when done
Terminado

YOU CAN MAKE *Deaf Welcome*

Learn American Sign Language

car • carro

YOU CAN MAKE *DeafWelcome*

How did you use this sign with the Deaf?
¿Cómo se utiliza esta señal con los sordos?

Explain • Explica

☐ (√) Check when done
Terminado

YOU CAN MAKE *Deaf Welcome*

Learn American Sign Language

walk • caminar

YOU CAN MAKE *DeafWelcome*

How did you use this sign with the Deaf?
¿Cómo se utiliza esta señal con los sordos?

Explain • Explica

_____

_____

_____

_____

_____

_____

☐ (√) Check when done
Terminado

YOU CAN MAKE *Deaf Welcome*

Learn American Sign Language

run • carrera

YOU CAN MAKE *DeafWelcome*

How did you use this sign with the Deaf?
¿Cómo se utiliza esta señal con los sordos?

Explain • Explica

_____

_____

_____

_____

_____

_____

(√) Check when done
Terminado

YOU CAN MAKE *Deaf Welcome*

Learn American Sign Language

home • casa

YOU CAN MAKE *DeafWelcome*

How did you use this sign with the Deaf?
¿Cómo se utiliza esta señal con los sordos?

Explain • Explica

_____

_____

_____

_____

_____

_____

☐ (√) Check when done
Terminado

YOU CAN MAKE *Deaf Welcome*

Learn American Sign Language

school • escuela

YOU CAN MAKE *DeafWelcome*

How did you use this sign with the Deaf?
¿Cómo se utiliza esta señal con los sordos?

Explain • Explica

_____

_____

_____

_____

_____

_____

☐ (√) Check when done
Terminado

YOU CAN MAKE *Deaf Welcome*

Learn American Sign Language

sick • enfermo(a)

YOU CAN MAKE *DeafWelcome*

How did you use this sign with the Deaf?
¿Cómo se utiliza esta señal con los sordos?

Explain • Explica

___

___

___

___

___

___

(√) Check when done
Terminado

YOU CAN MAKE *Deaf Welcome*

Learn American Sign Language

fine • bien

YOU CAN MAKE *DeafWelcome*

How did you use this sign with the Deaf?
¿Cómo se utiliza esta señal con los sordos?

Explain • Explica

_____

_____

_____

_____

_____

_____

_____

(√) Check when done
Terminado

YOU CAN MAKE *Deaf Welcome*

Learn American Sign Language

food allergies • alergias alimentarias

YOU CAN MAKE *DeafWelcome*

How did you use this sign with the Deaf?
¿Cómo se utiliza esta señal con los sordos?

Explain • Explica

_____

_____

_____

_____

_____

_____

(√) Check when done
Terminado

YOU CAN MAKE *Deaf Welcome*

Learn American Sign Language

"W"

water • agua

YOU CAN MAKE *DeafWelcome*

How did you use this sign with the Deaf?
¿Cómo se utiliza esta señal con los sordos?

Explain • Explica

_____

_____

_____

_____

_____

_____

(√) Check when done
Terminado

YOU CAN MAKE *Deaf* Welcome

Learn American Sign Language

"J"

juice • juicio

YOU CAN MAKE *DeafWelcome*

How did you use this sign with the Deaf?
¿Cómo se utiliza esta señal con los sordos?

Explain • Explica

_____

_____

_____

_____

_____

_____

☐ (√) Check when done
Terminado

YOU CAN MAKE *Deaf Welcome*

Learn American Sign Language

promise • promesa

YOU CAN MAKE *DeafWelcome*

How did you use this sign with the Deaf?
¿Cómo se utiliza esta señal con los sordos?

Explain • Explica

_____

_____

_____

_____

_____

_____

☐ (√) Check when done
Terminado

YOU CAN MAKE *Deaf Welcome*

Learn American Sign Language

work • trabajo

YOU CAN MAKE *DeafWelcome*

How did you use this sign with the Deaf?
¿Cómo se utiliza esta señal con los sordos?

Explain • Explica

_____

_____

_____

_____

_____

_____

☐ (√) Check when done
Terminado

YOU CAN MAKE *Deaf Welcome*

Learn American Sign Language

play • jugar

YOU CAN MAKE *DeafWelcome*

How did you use this sign with the Deaf?
¿Cómo se utiliza esta señal con los sordos?

Explain • Explica

_____

_____

_____

_____

_____

_____

_____

☐ (√) Check when done
Terminado

YOU CAN MAKE *Deaf Welcome*

Learn American Sign Language

police • policia

YOU CAN MAKE *DeafWelcome*

How did you use this sign with the Deaf?
¿Cómo se utiliza esta señal con los sordos?

Explain • Explica

_____

_____

_____

_____

_____

_____

☐ (√) Check when done
Terminado

YOU CAN MAKE *DeafWelcome*

Learn American Sign Language

fireman • bombero(a)

YOU CAN MAKE *DeafWelcome*

How did you use this sign with the Deaf?
¿Cómo se utiliza esta señal con los sordos?

Explain • Explica

_____

_____

_____

_____

_____

_____

(√) Check when done
Terminado

YOU CAN MAKE *Deaf Welcome*

Learn American Sign Language

call (telephone) • llámar

About the Author

Author, award-winning producer, director, interpreter and Sign Language TV Talk Show host, Theressa DuBois, affectionately called the *"Signing Oprah,"* has spent many years mentoring, coaching and training the Deaf and Hard-of-hearing in a variety of industries.

She established the Deaf Welcome Foundation, in 2004, to ensure the Deaf and Hard-of-hearing have equal access to mainstream products, services and amenities through signed TV programs, videos and special events. Her passion for the Deaf is undeniable, as she spearheads the ILY Television Network and entertains groups at speaking engagements across the country.

"You Can Make Deaf Welcome, Learn American Sign Language" is the first in a series of Deaf Welcome reference guides to promote communication, hospitality and Deaf inclusion. Teachers, shop owners, actors and students are encouraged to purchase these books and strive to put a smile on the face of your Deaf neighbors, customers, students, and friends, when you sign and make Deaf welcome in your everyday and at your special events.

Sales from this book supports the Deaf Welcome Foundation, the 501(c)(3) National Charity for Sign Language TV, Media and Film, as well as the ILY Television Network. Thank you for your donations, gifts, and grants to make Deaf welcome because "separate is never equal."
www.deafwelcome.org

CPSIA information can be obtained
at www.ICGtesting.com
Printed in the USA
LVHW07n0353120918
589889LV00007B/40/P